AI IMMORALITY

PHILIP TERRY

ADVANCED IMMORALITY

∼ ∨ ≡ ⊃

if p then q classics

40 Cranbourne Road, Old Trafford, Manchester, M16 9PZ

www.ifpthenq.co.uk
ifpthenq@fsmail.net
0161 872 5486

Published by *if p then q*

if p then q classics is part of the wider *if p then q* family

© Philip Terry 2012

ISBN 978-0-9571827-0-7

TABLE OF CONTENTS

50½ Crime Novels for Beginners	9
Advanced Immorality	21
First Steps in Phonology	41
Hamlet	44
Clop Clop	48
Days	50
A Berlin Notebook	59

To Ann and Lou

50½ CRIME NOVELS FOR BEGINNERS

It begins with the body in the lake. At first police dismiss it as an accident. Two more bodies appear. The lake is fenced off. Bodies continue to appear.

A man's upper body is found on a bench, wrapped in blankets. Later, a man's lower body is found, cut into pieces and deposited in six holdalls, left in lay-bys along the A12. Medical examination reveals that the body parts all belong to the same man. Baffled, police set up a mobile centre to gather information. After six months they have got nowhere and the centre is closed down.

The first sign that something is amiss is when the landlord discovers a bath full of pickled babies in an empty flat. Suspicion falls on the previous occupant, Marina Smith, a chemistry student from Markinch, currently on a gap year in the US. Medical examination reveals that the babies are quadruplets, drowned at birth, then preserved in formaldehyde. Police attempts to trace Smith lead nowhere, until an anonymous tip-off leads them to an isolated beach hut on Long Island. Police marksmen surround it.

It begins with the body in the lake. Immediately, the lake is dredged, but all that turns up is a rotted and illegible filofax. Nonetheless, the filofax supplies an important clue – DNA evidence leads investigators to a man selling knock-off stationery at a car boot sale in Wolverhampton. There is nothing to connect the man to the murder inquiry but he is charged with handling stolen goods. The case remains open.

It kicks off at Tesco's with the eyeball in the oxtail soup. A week later, an ear turns up in a portion of fresh pasta. A week after that, a toe is discovered in a sausage roll. Baffled, police set up a mobile centre to gather information. They are getting nowhere, when the manager of a rival store, limping, turns himself in.

It all starts when she misses the bus and takes a minicab instead. Later, her body is found dumped in a landfill site, the heart having been carefully removed. Investigation leads nowhere until the minicab is spotted on CCTV. A police raid on the driver's home while he is out reveals a freezer full of human body parts. Hiding all traces of the search, police marksmen surround the building.

It begins with the body in the lake. Later, a body is found dumped in a landfill site. Two more bodies appear, one in a ditch, one in a breaker's yard. Baffled, police set up a mobile centre to gather information. The bodies continue to appear.

It kicks off with the eyeballs in the oxtail soup. Later, a body is found, cut into pieces and deposited in six holdalls, left in lay-bys along the A12; the eyeballs are missing. Investigation leads nowhere, until a private eye is hired by the victim's family. He traces the holdalls and the soup tins to a garage in Essex. Police marksmen surround it.

There is a phone call in the night. A week later, an ear turns up in a jiffy bag, carefully wrapped in cotton wool. Seeing no alternative, the diplomat agrees to pay the exorbitant ransom. As instructed, he leaves the money in six identical holdalls in the toilets of a transit café. Police marksmen surround it.

The man's body is found on a bench, wrapped in blankets. At first police dismiss it as an accident. Two more bodies appear. The bench is fenced off. Bodies continue to appear.

It begins with the body in the lake. Forensic examination of the layer of mud sandwiched between the victim's skin and clothing reveals traces of semen and a fish supper. Detectives trace the origin of the fish supper to Harry's Plaice, where police fruitlessly examine CCTV footage, as management policy is to leave the system switched off at all times. Attempts to trace the origin of the semen also lead detectives to Harry's Plaice, where it turns out to be the secret ingredient in Harry's award-winning batter. The case remains open, though Harry's Plaice has been closed.

It starts with a hit and run involving a stolen minicab. A mother and her identical twin daughters, Petal and Rose, are killed instantly. Investigation leads nowhere, until the minicab is spotted on CCTV. Police trace it to a garage in Putney where the culprit, panicking, pulls out a gun and takes WPC Brown hostage. Police marksmen surround the building.

There is a phone call in the night. Immediately the lake is dredged, but all that turns up is a rotted and illegible filofax. There is another phone call. This time the garden is dug up; a human head is discovered hidden in a pot of basil. It is the first clue to solving the ten gruesome killings which will soon come to be known as the Decameron murders.

It kicks off with the eyeball in the oxtail soup. At first police dismiss it as an accident. Two more eyeballs appear, one in a tin of cream of tomato, one in a minestrone. The soup tins are traced to an isolated nightclub near Thaxted, which has been closed until further notice. The club is cordoned off. Eyeballs continue to appear.

It begins with the muddied corpses in the lake. A week later a man is found buried head first in the sand. After a lull of a month, another body is found, lodged inside the trunk of a hollow tree. It is at this point that PC Warner, a former literature student, points out the resemblance between the methods of killing and certain cantos of Dante's *Inferno*. PC Warner's immediate superior dismisses the remarks without a thought, until a further three corpses are discovered burnt to a crisp in an industrial incinerator, on which have been sprayed the words: "All hope abandon ye who enter in."

The girl's mutilated body is found in a dodgem car; on her back, carved with a knife, "Poles go home." Police are swift to respond, doubling the number of patrols and advising Polish women not to go out alone. Later, the body of another girl is found dumped in a landfill site, "Poles out" scored on her forehead. Police impose a curfew on Poles in the town centre after dark. Bodies continue to appear.

The first sign that something is amiss is when the toenail is discovered in the kebab. At first police dismiss it as an accident. Then a finger turns up in the taramasalata. A dawn raid on the restaurant with JCBs reveals that it is a front for a £50,000,000 a year cocaine business; a search of the basement quickly reveals the mutilated bodies of three members of a rival gang in a deep freeze. Four of the dealers are arrested, but the gang leader escapes, fleeing to Brazil.

It begins with the dismembered body of the prostitute in the wheelie bin. Suspicion first falls on Jed, her jealous lover and pimp, until Jed's body is found dumped in a sewer. Two more bodies appear. Baffled, police set up a mobile centre to gather information. Bodies continue to appear.

It starts with the body of the creative writing student in the lake. At first police dismiss it as an accident, until a tip-off directs them towards an online crime novel, where the drowning of a creative writing student by a serial killer is described in lurid detail. The next day, another body of a creative writing student is found, this time in a copse, again following a pattern described in the novel. Police trace the website to an isolated bungalow in Kent, home to failed novelist and ex-creative writing student Dan Rooney, and make their way to the house in haste, hoping to arrive in time to prevent any further loss of life. Marksmen surround the building.

It kicks off with the severed head of the dog in the washing machine. As a wave of copycat crimes sweep across the country, animal welfare groups are appalled, while canine insurance goes through the roof. Investigation leads nowhere, until a private eye is hired, paid for by an anonymous dog lover. A trail leads to the headquarters of Aviva, but nothing can be proved. On the verge of a breakthrough, the private eye disappears without trace, leaving an empty file in the back of his car and a blank laptop.

It starts with the discovery of the body of Penelope Burns-Templeton aka Donna Butcher at the Faber Academy crime writing retreat. Suspicion first falls on Maggie Motion, her bitterest rival, until Maggie's body is found slowly cooking in the Aga the following morning. Detectives place everyone on house arrest, while the course tutor, RJ Ellory, tries to calm students down, encouraging them to treat it as a hands-on creative writing exercise. Students exchange their solutions to the mystery as, one by one, they are picked off by the killer in their midst. On the final evening the guest writer arrives to give a reading in front of the survivors – it is Penelope Burns-Templeton, who reveals the whole series of events as a hoax.

It begins with the dismembered body of the prostitute in the wheelie bin. For a month, all goes quiet, then another body is found, also that of a prostitute, cut into pieces and deposited in six holdalls, left in lay-bys along the A12. CCTV footage leads police to hunt for a brown Ford Sierra registration number BO75 RHA. After a public call for help the Sierra is traced to a house in Sutton. Police marksmen surround it.

The first sign that something is amiss is when the body of a don is discovered floating in the Cam. At first police dismiss it as an accident; then the post-mortem reveals that the man was already dead before his body entered the water. Investigation reveals that the don was having an affair with one of his students, Jess Morley; suspicion falls on her ex-boyfriend Alfie. Police pursue Alfie to his lodgings but find that he has been missing ever since the day of the killing; then his body is found in the river. Detectives draw the obvious conclusion – that Alfie, having murdered his girlfriend's lover, has taken his own life – until a post-mortem reveals that he was already dead before his body entered the water.

It starts – though only later will this come to light – with the polonium-210 in the chicken korma. The following morning, the three students who ate it are all violently sick, brushing it off as another bad curry experience; only later, when they begin to lose their hair and their teeth, do they go to the doctor's and then to the police. It is at this point that medical teams find traces of the toxin polonium-210 in the blood of all three students, and a trail is uncovered which leads to the curry house. Detectives find that Russian émigré Professor Vladimir Vernitski, who had been giving a talk about the demise of democracy in Putin's Russia at the university, had also been dining in the curry house that evening, and guess that the polonium-210 had been intended for him. The condition of all three students rapidly deteriorates. They are buried in the grounds of the university. No formal apology is forthcoming from the Kremlin.

It begins with the body of the cross-dressing serial killer Martyn Carver in the ditch, his/her throat slit and hands cut off. Building up a profile of the victim, police notice that the manner of death bears a close resemblance to that Carver inflicted on his/her victims in the 1970s. Before the investigation has got very far, another body appears, also that of a serial killer, Ron Waites, recently released from Broadmoor; his body is found with the inner organs carefully removed, curried, and placed in a picnic basket next to his feet, a manner of death closely resembling that Waites inflicted on his five Asian victims in the 1980s. It does not take police long to see the extraordinary nature of the case on their hands – that of a serial killing of serial killers – and experts are assembled from all forces. As they make their public announcements, and carry out interviews and set up safe houses for serial killers, ex-serial killers, serial serial killers, and their families, or, in the case of serial monogamists, their partners and ex-partners, bodies continue to appear.

It starts with a leaked email revealing the whereabouts of the registered paedophile. Locals protest, standing outside his house with banners; a brick is thrown through his front window. The man is given police protection, but the protests continue. One night, armed with torches and baseball bats, a posse of young mothers descends on the house and sets it ablaze. Police arrive only in time to see the man, now a human fireball, hurl himself desperately from an upstairs window; he is dead on impact with the ground.

It kicks off when the cat, Sherman, is shot through the head with a handgun. Police treat the incident as low priority until the dog is discovered, also shot through the head. 24 hour CCTV is set up round the house and garden, but this doesn't stop the killer from entering the house undetected and dispatching the daughter, Lottie, again with a bullet through the head. Baffled, detectives place the house under constant surveillance, but this doesn't stop the killer from entering undetected and dispatching Lottie's mother, again with the trademark bullet through the head. The next day, to everyone's surprise, Lottie's father confesses to the crimes, saying he was bored with the routine of family life. As he awaits trial, a killer enters his cell undetected and shoots him through the head with a handgun.

It starts with the girl strangled halfway through her cornflakes by a man dressed as Tony the Tiger. Almost immediately the press brand him the "cereal" killer, though his second victim, again strangled at breakfast, is a nine-year-old boy eating toast. Investigation leads nowhere, until the "cereal" killer is caught on CCTV removing his Tiger costume. Quickly, police rush out a picture of the man, hoping to catch him before he strikes again. The murders stop, but the "cereal" killer himself is never caught.

It begins with the discovery of the body bricked up in the wall of the Castle Museum. At first it is thought to be an archaeological find, until forensic teams determine the date of decease to be circa 1963. The body turns out to be that of Yvonne Cooper, who disappeared mysteriously in the early 1960s on her way home from school. Detective work reveals that at around the same time, a group of Italian archaeologists had been involved in excavations in the same site, under the supervision of Giovanni Succhi, a name which turns out to have been false. The case remains open.

On the eve of the Darts World Championship, Martin Haas, the hot favourite, is shot through both legs on his way home from work, and forced to withdraw. Suspicion first falls on Topper "180" Harris, his bitterest rival, but police are unable to find any conclusive evidence. In a final attempt to nail Harris police raid his house, where they find 2kg of cocaine hidden in a copper kettle and £60,000 in cash; Harris is arrested on suspicion of drug trafficking and forced to withdraw from the tournament. In court Harris protests his innocence and produces CCTV footage of two men placing the money and cocaine in his house in an attempt to frame him; the case collapses. In a dramatic twist of events, it turns out that Haas, losing his nerve, has engineered the whole series of events in an attempt to ruin his rival; now confined to a wheelchair, police make an easy arrest.

It starts with a leaked email, suggesting malpractice at the nursery. At first police dismiss it, until another email arrives with an attachment showing a group of naked children. At once officers descend on the nursery, making several arrests. As they search the premises they uncover over 1,000 indecent images of children on a laptop, and a bricked up cellar. A month later, excavations in the cellar area uncover the bodies of three girls, whose disappearance, 30 years ago, had never been explained.

It kicks off with the body of the creative writing student in the lake. As a wave of copycat crimes sweep across the country, departments of creative writing are placed on red alert, while applications plummet. Investigation leads nowhere, until a private eye is hired, paid for by an anonymous donor. A trail leads to Faber and Faber, who have been launching their Writing Academy, but nothing can be proved. On the verge of a breakthrough, the private eye disappears without trace, leaving an empty file in the back of his car and a blank laptop.

It starts with a leaked email revealing the whereabouts of the registered paedophile. Locals protest, standing outside his house with banners; a brick is thrown through his front window. The man is given police protection, but the protests continue. One night, armed with torches and baseball bats, a posse of young mothers descends on the house and sets it ablaze. Police arrive only to see the man emerge from the garden shed, unscathed, as the young mothers, helplessly searching him out in the house, are burnt to a cinder.

It begins with the severed head of the dog in the washing machine. Police are swift to respond, doubling the number of patrols, and advising dog owners not to leave their pets alone. Nevertheless, the initial crime is repeated in an increasing number of houses, leaving the town's dog owners in a state of terror. Investigation leads nowhere, until forensic teams, taking DNA samples from all eleven washing machines, identify a common strand which points to the home of Ms Martha Bulridge, a known anti-fouling campaigner. Police surround the building, as WPC Brown persuades Ms Bulridge to come quietly.

There is a phone call in the night. A week later a man is found buried head first in the sand. There is another phone call. Police trace it to a garage in Kent where the culprit, panicking, pulls out a gun and takes two policewomen hostage. Police marksmen surround the building.

The first sign that something is amiss is when the toenail is discovered in the kebab. At first police dismiss it as an accident. Then a finger turns up in the taramasalata. Investigation leads nowhere until a private eye is hired, paid for by an anonymous kebab lover, who uncovers a trail leading to the mansion of Jon Ong, a rival fast food entrepreneur, who runs a chain of Chinese takeaways. Police surround the building, as two officers persuade Mr Ong to come quietly.

It begins with the body of a don floating in the Cam. For a month, all goes quiet, then another body is found, also that of a don, lying on its front in a punt. Two more bodies appear. Baffled, police set up a mobile centre to gather information. Bodies continue to appear.

It starts when the cat, Sherman, is shot through the head with a handgun. As a wave of copycat crimes sweeps across the country, animal welfare groups are appalled, and cat insurance rockets. Investigation leads nowhere, until a private eye is hired, paid for by an anonymous cat lover. A trail is uncovered leading to the rural squat of a hardcore vegan collective, who have masterminded the operation, hoping to destabilize the cat food industry. Police marksmen surround the squat.

The first sign that something is amiss is when the landlord discovers a bath full of pickled babies in an empty flat. Suspicion falls on Topper "180" Harris, the previous occupant of the flat, until an anonymous email implicates the ground floor nursery, Sure Start. At once officers descend on the nursery, but no arrests are made. Forensic examinations, meanwhile, reveal the perfectly preserved bodies to be those of Anglo-Saxons from the 8th century, ritually killed and preserved in bog water. The bodies, which had been missing for two years, are returned to the Local History Museum.

It starts with the body of the creative writing student in the lake, the toe of the left foot missing. Immediately, the lake is dredged for the toe, but all that turns up is a rotted and illegible filofax. A week later, a toe is discovered in a sausage roll in the refectory; on examination, however, it turns out to be the toe from a right foot. Baffled, police set up a mobile centre outside the library to gather information. The case remains open.

The girl's mutilated body is found in a dodgem car; on her back, carved with a knife, "Poles go home." As a wave of copycat crimes sweep across the country, Polish communities are placed on red alert, while immigration applications plummet. Investigation leads nowhere, until a private eye is hired, paid for by an anonymous donor, a Polish RAF veteran. A paper trail leads to a rightwing think tank, Britain Back on Track, but nothing can be proved. On the verge of a breakthrough, the body of the private eye is discovered in his car, having died from a heart attack; the files on his laptop are blank.

It starts when she misses the bus and takes a minicab instead. A week later, an ear turns up, delivered by courier, along with a ransom demand. Seeing no alternative, her parents agree to pay the ransom. As instructed, they make the exchange in a National Trust car park; but unbeknown to them they have been followed by plain clothes police officers. As the kidnappers make their getaway, police officers block the exits.

It begins with a hit and run involving a stolen minicab on a zebra crossing. As a wave of copycat crimes sweep across the country, minicab drivers are placed on red alert, while use of zebra crossings plummet. Investigation leads nowhere until the original minicab is spotted on CCTV. A police raid on the driver's home when he is out reveals nothing. Hiding all traces of the search, police marksmen surround the building.

It starts with the discovery of the body of the poet laureate at the Arvon Centre. At once police confiscate all the poetry written during the course and take it away as evidence. Under the supervision of Chief Inspector Bloom, extensive analysis of the manuscripts is carried out which reveals an almost universal and barely concealed Oedipal rivalry between the would-be poets and the laureate, which immediately places the whole cohort under suspicion, with the exception of Robert Hugill. Extensive interviewing leads nowhere, until forensic teams taking DNA samples from across the cohort identify the killer as none other than Hugill. As he is led away, asked why he committed the crime, Hugill comments: "I can't stand his poetry."

It begins with the discovery of the child's body bricked up in the wall of the convent. Locals protest, standing outside the convent with banners; a brick is thrown through a stained glass window. The Abbess is given police protection, but the protests continue. Detective work reveals that the body is that of the child novice Gunnhilda, said to have been murdered by Viking raiders in 844, though they are unable to explain the perfect preservation of the corpse. The Abbess offers up prayers to the Virgin Mary and petitions for Gunnhilda to be canonized.

On the eve of the world pole dancing tournament, Jenny Hill, the hot favourite, is shot in the head while out jogging. Suspicion first falls on Tony, her jealous lover, until Tony's body is found dumped in a skip. The spotlight now falls on Sally Carver, her bitterest rival, until Sally's body is found strangled in her hotel room. Attempting to prevent any further killings, police close down the tournament. Bodies continue to appear.

It begins with the body of the ex-para, a veteran of Bloody Sunday, floating in the Colne. At first police dismiss the drowning as an accident, until a rogue IRA cell claims responsibility. Investigation leads nowhere, until Barry McElroy, the leader of the cell, is accidentally caught on CCTV. Detectives trace him to a hideout in Basildon. Police marksmen surround the building.

The man's body is found on a bench wrapped in blankets. Suspicion first falls on his estranged boyfriend, Max, until Max's body is found drowned in his bath. Investigation leads nowhere, until a private eye is hired, paid for by an anonymous gay rights activist. The private eye uncovers a series of clues which implicate a Christian B&B network, recently fined £100,000 for discrimination against gay couples, but nothing can be proved. The case remains open.

There is a phone call in the night. A week later an eyeball turns up in the oxtail soup. Seeing no alternative, the soup manufacturers agree to pay. As instructed, the money is left in six identical soup tins in the toilets of a transit café. Police marksmen surround it.

It begins with the dismembered body of the butcher in the wheelie bin. For a month, all goes quiet, then another body is found, also that of a butcher, again dumped in a wheelie bin. Investigation leads nowhere, until a private eye is hired, paid for by an anonymous donor. A trail is uncovered leading to the rural squat of a hardcore vegan collective, who have masterminded the operation, hoping to destabilize the meat industry. Three of the vegans are arrested, but the squat founder, Matt, escapes to a Buddhist retreat in Tibet.

It starts with the body in the lake. Despite extensive investigation police are unable to find any suspects. The case remains open.

ADVANCED IMMORALITY

Grey moon	Grey sun	Black hole
	Angular anonymity	
Brown weed	Weak plastic	Dim foreground
	Crude language	
Untrimmed hedges	Dwarf chickens	Cornered field mouse
	Haphazard wrens	

A cat
purrs
under the table
A brief twittering
in the air
slowly
fades

White moon	Green Adonis	White dwarf
	Angular anonymity	

Sentient foot	Radiant foot	Light foot
	Unsuspecting foot	
Unmarked foot	Unmarked foot	Unmarked foot
	Defacing foot	
Sticky tar	Crushed bones	Muted cover-up
	Illiterate foot	

Yesterday's

erudite

chickens

betray

the iron rivers

to permafrost

and wilderness

Dangling rope	Rising pepper	Resident dog
	Betraying foot	

Colourful pensioners	Crossbred pigeons	Silenced ducks
	Sexed animals	
Tinny whistles	Steady hatred	Staple fodder
	Equilateral holidays	
Improper nicknames	Opaque surnames	Legitimate first names
	Divergent deaths	

The trilobite
lies fixed
under the clay
On top of
the stump
herbs
wither

Silenced whistles	Tinny hates	Steady ducks
	Old-fashioned consonants	

Molten butterflies	Unadorned power cuts	Silent mists
	Sympathetic glances	
Rectangular moths	Precise lines	Glistening soil
	Isolated glances	
Virgin bushes	Swaying branches	Dressed leaves
	Urbane glances	

There is more oil
beneath the soil
but the tanker
of sweet intoxicants
comes home slowly
by rail
at dawn

Stagnated woods	Unified ranges	Smooth lakes
	Sympathetic glances	

Cultivated wheat	Rough ruby	Feathery gorse
	Nearby town	
Damaged worm	Opaque sapphire	Black laburnum
	Navel caves	
Still darkroom	Invisible silk	Feathery gorse
	Nearby town	

The air raid shelter
in the back garden
is never there for long
The temple's foundations
are rotten
the worshipper bare
in the palpable still air

Feathery wheat	Rough ruby	Cultivated gorse
	Disembodied laburnum	

Alert deserts	Scorched wastelands	Arid plains
	Persistent drought	
Dying roots	Desiccated seeds	Deluded buds
	Alert deserts	
Red streams	Open combat	Settled dust
	Persistent forgetfulness	

Reaching
the special tank
the metal sinks
towards gleaming
You mustn't
fall into
the acid bath

Purple stilts	Camouflaged tanks	Horizontal bullets
	City in mourning	

Green squatter	Modern figures	Common marks
	Eclipsing moon	
Sparse letters	Empty pages	Thin verses
	Sweet-smelling sun	
Unopened CD-roms	Prototype CD-roms	Sealed CD-roms
	Bright earth	

He no longer bothers
to look down at
the mountain of sludge
the grey worms
the spread-out plastic
the unsought-for shards
He sees none of it

Unopened CD-roms	Prototype CD-roms	Sealed CD-roms
	Sinking moon	

Clear sky	Constant stream	Pure earth
	Cultivated ponds	
Held hips	Polished ceilings	Straight threads
	Mundane milkshakes	
Uneaten iron	Regurgitated gold	Lemonade stalls
	Plastic pills	

The rarefaction

of the perfume

the brightness

of the colouring

the stillness

of the

sundial

Film-wrapped sandwiches	Ironed diets	Abstemious ponds
	Nuptial stalls	

Crude breakers	Fresh pimento	Tangled rings
	Blissful returns	
Steamed envelopes	Empty solos	Lost letters
	Inane returns	
Artless flower	Dull handbags	Perfect corks
	Architectural returns	

A full
liner stops
slowly stops
upstream from
Southend
Sheerness
Gravesend

Dull stamps	Artificial intelligence	Pristine belt
	Architectural returns	

Rapid drowsiness	Unreal reality	Rapid evening
	Harmless enmity	
Rapid evening	Realised dream	Unsung midnight
	Fluctuating moon	
Concentrated individual	Extraordinary weeds	Clenched fists
	Expansive day	

Here there are
no roadblocks
no sounds
no towers
Hawthorn bushes
mark the
field's edge

Rapid mourning	Glowing moon	Fertile breakfast
	Intense day	

Empty sun	Purple sun	Weightless sun
	Shrunk horizon	
Light snow	Sporadic snow	Soft snow
	Desiccated moon	
Advancing drought	Static drought	Advanced drought
	Shrivelled sun	

                The windy dried-
                up river bed
                is silent,
                its mouth empty
                It is too bright
                above the lizard's
                shadeless hole

Thin streams	Stoic streams	Uncommon streams
	Spring moons	

Quiet school	Polished doorknob	January snows
	Germinating seeds	
Uncensored reports	Basic vocabulary	Lighthearted sentences
	Black roots	
Rising moon	Pacifist moon	Cloud-covered moon
	Short nights	

At the start of the day
the unemployed steal
discarded rubbish
At the end of the day
leafless philosophical
maxims
shrink

Old concrete	Rising sap	January snows
	Finishing school	

Static cat	Purring cat	Scratching cat
	Wild cat	
Static dog	Growling dog	Panting dog
	Wild dog	
Static rabbit	Purring tiger	Purple gorilla
	Wild goldfish	

On safari
the blind traveller
listens out for
animal noises
On the crowded plain
a swarm of flies
breeds on dung

Static mouse	Jumping frog	Stationary wasp
	Wild eagle	

Restrained silence	Colourless modesty	Synthetic cube
	Lone snowdrop	
Anorexic vanity	Suffocating modesty	Sensible cube
	Iridescent snowdrop	
Suffocating arms	Modest whiteness	Simple steps
	Picked snowdrop	

Plastic steeples

sleepwalk the skies

A tin moon

sinks in the ocean

The sun's disc

comes too soon

too bright

Unimpeded tornado	Shouted instructions	Noisy reflections
	Perfect snowdrop	

Collected ash	Mellow pipes	Scarce cigarettes
	European trunks	
Defeated claustrophobia	Smooth waters	Slippery windscreens
	Sober silence	
Wide open veins	Impenetrable walls	Bored faces
	Prudish people	

After the green day
out of the sunlight
a teetotaller sits
in the pure air
of linen vests
of springs
of herbal cigarettes

Sleeping summer	Soporific rains	Minor acceptance
	Drawn out indecision	

Mundane viewing	Esoteric show	Banal proximities
	Suburban rest	
Pilot house	Still swan	Pure river
	Suburban rest	
Mineral magnet	Humble dwellings	Alcoholic homes
	Suburban rest	

Sitting at windows
princesses always
disappear slowly
well-known princesses
whose static uncertainty
the hasty house servant
too easily deciphers

Rebuilt railways	Arriving horses	Sea routes
	Envisioned cul-de-sacs	

Searing hate	Rusty helmet	Soft shirt
	Migrant memories	
Raw passion	Warm anonymity	Textured glass
	Recovered memories	
Frozen hate	Inundated lake	Floating moons
	Industrial waste	

What is this absence of signs?
No slug trails
No cuckoo's song
No hoot of owl
What is this absence of signs?
Up here in the tower
plenitude dissolves

Searing hate	Migrant memories	Recovered forgetfulness
	Industrial waste	

City swan	Spring swan	Confident swan
	Modest hill	
Tame cygnet	Summer cygnet	Glossy cygnet
	Modest park	
Feminine support	Civilian support	Pacifist support
	Modest priest's hole	

In the courtyard
the witch has gone
away who otherwise
stoops as low
as the root
as the root
beneath the hut

Giant birdthings	Adult grams	Crude business
	Certain adulthood	

Bald planet   Religious commonplace   Unremarkable banality
                         Cheap water
Basic shave   Unremarkable moment   Transparent object
                         Bored foxes
Clean rain   Dehydrated cube   Inorganic fuel
                         Extraordinary sign

                         The sun escapes
                         the summit
                         Without a sound
                         a boulder
                         falls
                         Inside the ground
                         turns dark

Transparent cups   Delicate timpani   Infernal fires
                         Unreal maturity

Unworn suits	Physical negligés	Pristine actions
	Unvisited websites	
Unuttered things	Unwanted dinners	Physical core
	Airbrushed websites	
Polluted air	Sophisticated bartering	Perennial things
	Refreshed websites	

Unoxidised steel rivets
the locked safe
Modesty
hasn't marked
the prose
of the future
dénouement

Physical suits	Physical negligés	Perennial things
	Unvisited websites	

FIRST STEPS IN PHONOLOGY

I
Let's go surfing,
I'm learning Polish;
I like this lake.

How about a shower now?
I need more soap,
My nurse pokes her nose in my letters.

The coward crouched behind his car.
You have to bow your head to get into the bower;
You have to bow your head to get into the boa.

II
I left the car and Esther in his hands,
I'm tired of changing tyres.
They're arranging for a tour of the Pyrenees.

I bought toys for the four of them,
The way he leered at me was embarrassing.
The schooner was moored.

What on earth's that?
He complained about the tent;
He complained about the dent.

III
They were all alone,
She swore it was a load of lies.
Willie will never bet again.

Jack stuffed himself with buns,
Maggie blushed.
That was a hard month.

We can't understand the last part.
I want to buy this goat;
I want to buy this coat.

IV
Today's the fifth anniversary of our son Keith,
He's a rather uncouth youth,
Don't breathe a word to anybody about his death.

Henry prefers red roses,
He's the Chairman of Bath's Athletic Club.
Peter and Oliver are in the cafeteria.

Your vowel will sound better if you speak lower.
This book's my favourite choice;
This book's my favourite Joyce.

V
Myths are dead, they say, we won't miss them.
Ruth reminds me of her uncle Ralph,
His ruthless rule in rural areas raised uproar.

The landlord annoys me,
He clawed at me with his moist hands.
I roared at Roy and he roared back.

He tried to wrench the revolver from his grip.
They won't stop cheering;
They won't stop jeering.

VI
His hand hit her head inadvertently.
How harmful was it to her health?
Stop that hideous yawn of yours.

Where there used to be a plethora of good
Theatres, there is now a dearth of them.
Hooligans attack telephone booths.

Howard Hughes had a heart attack in his hotel.
The bombs jarred the building;
The bombs charred the building.

VII
There'll be no renewal of your allowance.
She shows more and more interest in rare engravings,
She takes care of her aunt.

Do you know any northern part of Britain?
Allowing for lack of practice,
I'd say you answered well.

They found a golden medal among the rubble.
They tug and tug;
They dug and dug.

VIII
Who has heard of Henry Hume,
The hairdresser from Hartley?
He haunted her house, howling in halls,

Hurling hard objects around,
Making her hair stand on end.
He didn't seem to bother about kith and kin.

The young couple happened to know our region.
I've bought these greengages;
I've brought these green cages.

IX
They were buttoned up to the chin:
Tell the steward we're all stewing in here,
Roy's writing an irritating riddle.

Our parson is partial to the bottle.
It was a dull Saturday;
The wind lashed relentlessly at the pier.

The bank's invested less than we expected.
They have no more guts;
They have no more cuts.

HAMLET

Seems, madam? Must I remember? And what make you from Wittenburg, Horatio? But what is your affair in Elsinore? Saw? Who? The King my father? But where was this? Did you not speak to it? Hold you the watch tonight? Armed, say you? What looked he? Frowningly? Pale or red? And fixed his eyes upon you? Stayed it long? His beard was grizzly, no? What hour now? What may this mean, that thou, dead corpse, again in complete steel, revisitst thus the glimpses of the moon, making night hideous, and we fools of nature so horridly to shake our disposition with thoughts beyond the reaches of our souls? Say, why is this? Wherefore? What should we do? Why, what should be the fear? I do not set my life at a pin's fee, and for my soul, what can it do to that, being a thing immortal as itself? Whither wilt thou lead me? What? Murder? Mine uncle? What else? And shall I couple hell? Remember thee? Remember thee? How say you then, would heart of man once think it? But you'll be secret? Ah ha, boy, sayst thou so? Art thou there, true penny? Canst work i' th' earth so fast? Have you a daughter? Between who? How dost thou, Guildenstern? Ah, Rosencrantz – good lads, how do ye both? Nor the soles of her shoe? Then thou live about her waist, or in the middle of her favour? In the secret parts of Fortune? What's the news? What have you, my good friends, deserved at the hands of Fortune that she sends you to prison hither? Shall we to th' court? What make you at Elsinore? Were you not sent for? Is it your own inclining? Is it a free visitation? And yet to me what is this quintessence of dust? Why did you laugh, then, when I said "Man delights not me"? What players are they? How chances it they travel? Do they hold the same estimation they did when I was in the city? Are they so followed? How comes it? Do they grow rusty? What, are they children? Who maintains 'em? How are they escorted? Will they pursue the quality no longer than they can sing? Will they not say afterwards, if they should grow themselves to common players – as it is like most will, if their means are not better – their writers do them wrong to make them exclaim against their own succession? Is't possible? Do the boys carry it away? Am I not i' th' right, old Jephthah? "The mobbled queen"? Good my lord, will you see the players well bestowed? Do ye hear? Use every man after his desert, and who should scape whipping? Dost thou hear me, old friend? Can you play the murder of Gonzago? You could for a need study a speech of some dozen or sixteen lines which I would set down and insert in't, could ye not? What's Hecuba to him, or he to Hecuba, that he should weep for her? What would he do had he the motive and the cue for passion that I have? Am I a coward? Who calls me villain, breaks my pate across, plucks off my beard and blows it in my face, tweaks me by th' nose, gives me the lie i' th' throat as deep as to the lungs? Who does me this? Ha? Why, what an ass am I? There's the respect that makes calamity of so long life, for who would bear the whips and scorns of time, th' oppressor's wrong, the proud man's contumely, the pangs of disprized love, the law's delay, the insolence of office, and the spurns that patient merit of th' unworthy takes, when he himself might his quietus make with a bare bodkin? Who would these fardels bear, to grunt and sweat under a weary life, but that the dread of something after death, the undiscovered country from whose bourn no traveller returns, puzzles the will, and makes us rather bear those ills we have than fly to others that we know not of? Ha, ha? Are you honest? Are you fair? Why wouldst thou be a breeder of sinners? What would such fellows as I do crawling between heaven and earth? Where's your father? How now, my lord? Will the King hear this piece of work? Will you two help to hasten then? Nay, do not think I flatter; for what advancement could I hope from thee, that no revenue hast but thy good spirits to feed and clothe thee? Why should the poor be flattered? Dost thou hear? And what did you enact? Be the players ready? Lady, shall I lie in your lap? I mean my head upon your lap? Do you think I meant country matters? Who, I? What should a man do but be merry? So long? Is this a prologue, or the posy of a ring? Madam, how like you this play? Marry, how? 'Tis a knavish piece of work; but what o' that? What, frightened with false fire? Would not this, sir, and a forest of feathers, if the rest of my fortunes turn Turk with me, with two Provençal roses on my razed shoes, get me a fellowship in a cry of players, sir? Didst perceive? Upon the talk of the pois'ning? Ay, sir, what of him? With drink, sir? My mother, you say? But is there no sequel at the heels of this mother's admiration? Have you any further trade with us? To withdraw with you, why do you go about to recover the wind of me as if you would drive me into a toil? Will you play upon this pipe? 'Sblood, do you think I am easier to be played on than a pipe? Do you see yonder cloud that's almost in shape of a camel? A took my father grossly, full of bread, with all his crimes broad blown, as flush as May; and how his audit stands, who knows save heaven? And am I then revenged to take him in the purging of his soul, when he is fit and seasoned for his passage? Now, mother, what's the matter? What's the matter now? How now, a rat? Is it the King? Have you eyes? Could you on this fair mountain leave to feed, and batten on this moor? Ha, have you eyes? You cannot call it love, for at your age the heyday in the blood is tame, it's humble, and waits upon the judgement; and what judgement would step from this to this? What devil was't that thus hath cozened you at hood-man blind? O shame, where is thy blush? What would you, gracious figure? Th' important acting of your dread command? How is it with you lady? Do you see nothing there? Nor did you nothing hear? Ecstasy? 'Twere good you let him know, for who that's but a queen, fair, sober, wise, would from a paddock, from a boat, a gib, such dear concernings hide? Who would do so? You know that? What noise? Who calls on Hamlet? Besides, to be demanded of a sponge – what replication should be made by the son of a king? For England? Has this fellow no feeling of his business that a sings at grave-making? This might be the pate of a politician which this ass o'er-offices, one that would circumvent God, might it not? How dost thou, good lord? This might be my lord such a one's horse when a meant to beg it, might it not? Did these bones cost no more the breeding but to play at loggats with 'em? Why might that not be the skull of a lawyer? Where be his quiddits now, his quillets, his cases, his tenures, and his tricks? Why does he suffer this rude knave now to knock him about the sconce with a dirty shovel, and will not tell him of his action of battery? Is this the fine of his fines and the recovery of his recoveries, to have his fine pate full of fine dirt? Will his vouchers vouch him no more of his purchases, and double ones too, than the length and breadth of a pair of indentures? The very conveyances of his lands will hardly lie in this box; and must th' inheritor himself have no more, ha? Is not parchment made of sheepskins? Whose grave's this sirrah?

What man dost thou dig it for? What woman, then? Who is to be buried in't? How long hast thou been a gravemaker? How long is that since? Ay, marry, why was he sent into England? Why? How came he mad? How strangely? Upon what ground? How long will a man lie i' th' earth ere he rot? Why he more than another? Whose was it? This? Where be your jibes now, your gambols, your songs, your flashes of merriment that were wont to set the table on a roar? Not one now to mock your own grinning? Quite chop-fallen? Dost thou think Alexander looked o' this fashion i' th' earth? Why may not imagination trace the noble dust of Alexander till a find it stopping a bung-hole? No, faith, not a jot; but to follow him thither with modesty enough, and likelihood to lead it, as thus: Alexander died, Alexander was buried, Alexander returned into dust, the dust is earth, of earth we make loam, and why of that loam whereto he was converted might they not stop a beer-barrel? Here comes the King, the Queen, the courtiers – who is that they follow, and with such maimed rites? What is he whose grief bears such an emphasis, whose phrase of sorrow conjures the wand'ring stars and makes them stand like wonder-wounded hearers? What wilt thou do for her? Woot weep, woot fight, woot fast, woot tear thyself, woot drink up eisel, eat a crocodile? Dost thou come here to whine, to outface me with leaping in her grave? Hear you, sir, what is the reason that you use me thus? You do remember all the cirumstance? But wilt thou hear me how I did proceed? Wilt thou know th' effect of what I wrote? Does it not, think'st thee, stand me now upon – he that hath killed my King and whored my mother, popped in between th' election and my hopes, thrown out his angle for my proper life, and with such coz'nage – is't not perfect conscience to quit him with this arm? And is't not to be damned to let this canker out of our nature come in further evil? Dost know this water-fly? What's his weapon? What call you the carriages? Why is this "imponed", as you call it? How if I answer no? Since no man has aught of what he leaves, what is't to leave betimes? Was't Hamlet wronged Laertes? Who does it then? These foils have all a length? How does the Queen? The point envenomed too? Is thy union here? What warlike noise is this?

CLOP CLOP

Gene clop rush clop hot clop lung clop
Hat clop hole clop cop clop cough clop
Cup clop rug clop bar clop burn clop
Wind clop fast clop cream clop hit clop
Denim clop hard clop cool clop black clop
Curb clop bucket clop wood clop glow clop

Wind clop mutant clop cell clop glow clop
Singe clop shadow clop pink clop lung clop
Early clop late clop shared clop black clop
First clop last clop rough clop cough clop
Light clop French clop Turkish clop hit clop
Old clop dry clop sex clop burn clop

Stale clop stubbed clop bed clop burn clop
Walk clop flight clop borrowed clop glow clop
Begged clop hidden clop secret clop hit clop
Bench clop soggy clop Dutch clop lung clop
Spanish clop strong clop filter clop cough clop
Gold clop maïs clop drag clop black clop

Drug clop death clop damp clop black clop
Camp clop boat clop beach clop burn clop
Half clop banned clop herbal clop cough clop
Caught clop busted clop flic clop glow clop
Job clop coffee clop beer clop black clop
Queer clop pub clop grub clop hit clop

Break clop snack clop breath clop hit clop
Cilia clop smooth clop sad clop black clop
Happy clop lucky clop toasted clop lung clop
Roasted clop ear clop pocket clop burn clop
Lit clop silent clop rushed clop glow clop
Savoured clop long clop short clop cough clop

Russian clop fatal clop funeral clop cough clop
Wedding clop birthday clop Christmas clop hit clop
Cliff clop cottage clop brand clop glow clop
Gangster clop palm clop bath clop black clop
Throat clop breath clop nose clop burn clop
Cloud clop night clop fight clop lung clop

Dry clop glow clop kick clop cough clop
Lift clop lung clop tent clop hit clop
Flat clop black clop prayer clop burn clop

DAYS

Days when you wish you could start all over again.

Days spent in meetings.

Days waiting for the ash clouds to pass.

Nights when you can't sleep.

Mornings when you stay in bed.

Mornings spent daydreaming, staring out the classroom window.

Mornings when you sing in the shower.

Mornings when the car doesn't start.

Afternoons spent in galleries, on the last day of the show, so crowded you can barely see the paintings.

Hours spent lying on my back, looking out for shooting stars.

Hours spent sitting in traffic jams, nervously watching the temperature gauge.

Hours spent marking exam papers, wishing you could be doing something else.

Hours spent drinking Abbot and St. Edmunds ("That's the damage boy.")

Hours wasted watching adverts.

Moments when you look in the mirror and see yourself getting older.

Moments when you resolve to stop drinking (which are soon forgotten).

Moments when you don't want to believe what you're hearing.

Moments when you can't believe what you're hearing.

Moments when only Debussy will do.

Moments when it has to be Keats.

Moments spent waiting for the bus.

Moments when you give up on the bus and decide to walk instead.

Moments watching vapour trails vanishing.

Moments listening to doves cooing.

Moments spent throwing up.

Days when everything seems pointless.

Days waiting for a house call that doesn't happen.

Days when you have to do something you don't want to and put it off.

Days facing the music.

Days when you run out of cat food.

Days when you are ill and take the day off work and feel better by lunchtime but still take the day off work.

Hours wasted driving.

Hours spent searching the internet for information you never find.

Hours spent washing up.

Hours spent sanding floorboards, wondering how much longer it could possibly take.

Hours filling in forms.

Nights when there's a sickle moon.

Nights when you make a packed lunch for the following day.

Nights at school discos.

Afternoons when you arrive at the station too early.

Afternoons at band practices.

Afternoons listening to Ligeti.

Afternoons spent taking down the Christmas tree.

Afternoons when you buy fish and chips.

Mornings when the bus is late.

Mornings when you get up in the dark.

Mornings when there's ice on the windscreen.

Mornings walking in fresh snow, the crunch of it compacting under your feet.

Mornings when your car breaks down, waiting for the AA.

Mornings of hesitation and doubt, not knowing what to get on with.

Mornings spent filling the car with junk, driving to the dump, only to find it closed.

Mornings spent decorating the Christmas tree.

Mornings stuck in traffic.

Mornings spent making homemade chutney.

Mornings spent answering emails.

Mornings spent at B&Q.

Mornings in bed thinking what colour to paint the walls.

Mornings when you catch the train early and think how glad you are you don't have to do this every day.

Mornings that begin with kippers.

Mornings writing.

Mornings when you've been up all night.

Moments waiting for someone to pass the joint.

Moments when you smell burning.

Moments that come only once.

Moments when you experience *déjà vu*.

Moments when you're sure you can feel the earth turn.

Moments picking food out of your teeth.

Moments of bitterness.

Afternoons playing rugby.

Afternoons watching television.

Afternoons when you stay in the bath till it's gone cold.

Afternoons dining out.

Afternoons in the garden, flicking through books, dozing in the sun.

Afternoons bunking off school.

Afternoons when you stop to look at the sunset and notice that it's a completely unrealistic amateur photographer pink.

Afternoons walking when you should be in a meeting.

Afternoons digging in the garden.

Days waiting for the sun to break through the clouds.

Days waiting for you to get better.

Death days.

Nights spent watching the election results come in.

Nights counting sheep.

Hours wasted watching football.

Hours planning holidays.

Hours translating Queneau.

Hours spent at airports, waiting for a delayed flight, reading the only book you have, which you wish you'd left at home.

Hours wasted trying to get tickets online.

Hours on the road, wondering when you're going to arrive.

Hours waiting for a hangover to pass.

Hours spent weeding.

Hours playing backgammon.

Hours spent doing jigsaws at Christmas.

Hours doing nothing.

Mornings watching disasters unfold on television.

Mornings when you'd rather not wake up.

Mornings when the bus arrives on time.

Mornings when the cat's sick.

Nights when you don't know what to cook.

Nights when you hear the ghost of your father on the stairs.

Nights when you hear fireworks.

Nights playing poker.

Nights being eaten by mosquitos.

Nights when someone pulls out a knife.

Moments when you find the *mot juste*.

Frisbee moments.

Days of unexpected sunshine.

Days when the holiday is coming to an end.

Days when nothing goes as planned.

Days of mourning.

Days when there's work on the line.

Days that seem to disappear before they have started.

Afternoons spent sewing zips on to trousers.

Afternoons getting stoned.

Afternoons picnicking by the river.

Afternoons soaking up the sun.

Afternoons when you plan to go out for a walk and it starts snowing, hard. You go out anyway – the beauty of the snow.

Afternoons watching Wimbledon.

Afternoons when you're overcome by inertia.

Hours frittered away.

Hours spent in A&E.

Hours spent sleeping.

Days spent reading Dante.

Days when you curse Cameron.

Days examining in Oxford.

Days winging it.

Days on holiday when everything works out.

Days when something happens that you don't hear about till later.

Days spent driving in the rain.

Days when you know you're not going to get any peace.

Mornings bunking off.

Mornings listening to the Diabelli Variations.

Mornings when a fuse blows.

Moments worrying about your liver.

Moments regretted.

Nights channel hopping.

Ginsberg nights.

Nights when your calf cramps up.

Nights at award ceremonies.

Nights spent camping by the creek.

Nights spent on LSD.

Nights waiting for the bus when you think it's never going to come.

Nights when you go out like a light.

Nights when you stay up all night.

Cold nights.

Nights spent travelling.

Noisy nights.

Nights spent in hotels.

Nights when you're sure you've seen a UFO.

Nights plotting the constellations.

Nights spent revising.

Nights at gigs.

Nights spent out of your head.

Afternoons when you let yourself eat cake.

Afternoons watching movies.

Afternoons waiting for the match.

Afternoons playing Howzat!

Afternoons cycle racing.

Hours making unnecessary journeys.

Hours when you can't put pen to paper.

Mornings waiting for the phone to ring.

Mornings when your well-laid plans quickly come unstuck.

Mornings when you need to put an extra hole in your belt.

Mornings that are one in a million.

Mornings of cold fog.

Mornings listening to Philip Glass.

Mornings when you get your eyes tested.

Mornings when you put a manuscript in the post.

Days out cycling.

Days spent dithering.

Days playing Subbuteo.

Days when you get on the wrong train.

Days building tree houses.

Days canoeing down the Dordogne.

Days spent arguing.

Days when the sweep comes and you see the brush poking out the top of the chimney.

A BERLIN NOTEBOOK

Black beetle. Rubble mountain. Cow parsley. Steel pylon. Red butterfly. Ski run. Tall poplar. Rusting Daimler. Blue graffiti. Tarmac track. Green beetle. Steel cable.

Traces of inner wall snake across a field: on one side blackberries grow, on one side elderflower.

Isolated tree. Smooth concrete. Dense undergrowth. Rich soil.

*

Ostentatious housing. Colourful bins. Pristine gardens. High fences. Closed footpaths. Private gardens. Karl-Marx-Strasse. Beautiful irony. Villa Mescala. Verdigris carport. Unprincipled development. Shady deals.

These private gardens which have stolen the public footpath, peopled only by gardeners.

Unprincipled development. Sawn up footpath. Private gardens. Dirty money.

*

Ornamental palace. Green bridge. Green bench. Gold lions. Gilded pagoda. Sudden laughter. Choppy water. Moored boat. Squeaking truck. Pointed camera. Falling leaf. Diving swallow.

A man sits on a bench, gazing at the water, smoking a cigarette. What is he thinking?

Empty bench. Palace garden. Cobbled road. Turning cyclists.

*

Fresh breeze. Tilting yacht. Clear sky. Fallen tree. Italian tower. Towering beech. Island chapel. Isolated bench. Passing cyclists. Collapsed bridge. Full sail. Occupied bench.

A fork in the road. Now the man I was following is following me.

Slippery steps. Tonsured jogger. Lakeside restaurant. Fish and wine.

*

Gusting wind. Swaying olive. Animated voices. Texting cyclist. Swirling leaves. Flying napkins. Mistaken order. Missed rendez-vous. Fleeing customers. Deserted table. Long walk. Tall buildings.

The waiter looks up into the sky. What is he staring at? A flying plastic bag.

Delayed rendez-vous. Disappointed pigeon. Efficient waiter. Incongruous ice cream.

Honky-tonk music. Run-down shack. Executive villa. Zen garden. Garden sculptures. Coiled hose. Barking dog. Open fields. Stacked logs. Turning vehicle. Pink villa. Concealed track.

So many tidying their gardens here: beyond the wall, people have settled into retirement.

Glum cyclist. White butterfly. Ardent jogger. Concealed sign.

*

Straight track. Distant jogger. Silent cyclist. Gentle breeze. Black dog. Pink tongue. Suspicious woman. Blue jeans. Noisy cyclists. Monotonous trees. Calling birds. Tired steps.

Monotony of the walk. Monotony of the border guard.

Straight track. Regular footfall. Hovering bee. Monotonous breeze.

*

Trotting dog. Flowering orchid. Ripening wheat. Standing man. Tree tunnel. Smooth trunks. Secret graffiti. Darkening sky. Balding cyclist. Occupied bench. Dilapidated map. Distant chimneys.

In the middle of nowhere, I stop and talk to two cyclists. One of them, it turns out, was formerly a border guard on this section of the wall. He is proud of the fact there were very few successful crossings at this point. Only one, in fact, his uncle.

Ripening maize. Diving swift. Ripe cherries. Bitter taste.

*

Twittering skylark. Crawling ants. Calling crow. Trotting dog. Busy road. Red lorry. Unripe apples. Gifted seeds. Distant tower blocks. Solitary magpie. Calling crickets. Mysterious poles.

Between rows of apple trees, every 20 metres or so, tall wooden poles with a "T" bar at the top. What are they for?

Light breeze. Yellow lorry. Red roof. Abandoned bag.

*

Incomprehensible conversation. Vigorous hand gestures. Comfortable benches. Parked bicycles. Black beetle. Yellow shirt. Struck-up conversation. Pointing finger. Calm conversation. Immaculate bicycle. Barking dog. Information panel.

Spray-paint covers the Information panel, necessitating talk.

Black paint. Full rubbish bin. Busy crossroads. Passing train.

German cars. A black one. A blue one. A grey one. A black one. German taxis. A cream one. Another cream one. German cars. A black one. Another black one. A white one.

Watching German cars, you would not miss much if you were colour blind.

German cars. Another grey one. German taxis. I think they are all cream.

*

Straight track. Light rain. Fluttering flag. Psychedelic geranium. Concrete wall. Pebble façade. Thai sushi. Brown caravan. Broken branch. Squeaking flag. Spanish tiles. Reversing truck.

They call this the "Shepherds' Meadow", but there are no shepherds around here.

Giant billboard. Garbage stink. Septic tanks. Industrial complex.

*

Tile track. Wooden track. Sand track. Grass track. Dry track. Muddy track. Gravel track. Cobbled track. Straight track. Flat track. Asphalt track. Glass track.

A wall remnant, the first of the day, stretching for two, three, four hundred metres. Among the messy graffiti, I can pick out only a name or two: Nathan Lewis, Alison Lewis.

Clay track. Curving track. Purple track. Forbidden track.

*

White daisies. Yellow daisies. Red poppies. Silver birch. Tall grasses. Wire fence. Passing traffic. Pristine bench. Grey bin. Young sapling. Dark pine. Passing helicopter.

A paved path here runs perpendicular to the wall, passing right through it where a panel has been removed.

Pristine bench. Simple transgression. Meadow flowers. Passing cyclist.

*

Blue plant. Giant crow. Yellow house. Yellow flower. Pink house. Noisy crow. Flying crow. Grafittied bench. Concealed motorway. Landscaped meadow. Wet bench. Scary crow.

Mother of all crows, plus mates. Yet clap your hands and they're off like a shot.

Flying crows. Fluttering crows. Grumpy dog walker. Silent crows.

*

Grazing land. Chestnut horses. Fat pylons. Whinnying horses. Private road. Large puddle. Pony trecking. Happy children. Landing jet. Cock crow. Wall lighting. Stinger nettle.

Everywhere new life takes hold in the former deathstrip.

Feeding goats. Chestnut horses. Flat fields. Turning car.

*

Straight track. Asphalt track. Straight track. Asphalt track. Straight track. Asphalt track. Straight track. Asphalt track. Straight track. Asphalt track. Straight track. Asphalt track.

My feet are hurting from pounding this straight asphalt track.

Straight track. Asphalt track. Straight track. Asphalt track.

*

Monotonous track. Featureless fields. Barely a sign of the wall. Tarmac track. Passing cyclists. Monotonous walk. Aggressive crows. Grey and black. Dark sky. Constant tread. Inappropriate footwear. Empty stomach.

So tired I'm beginning to sway on my feet – nearly get hit by a cyclist. I look back at him. He looks back at me. I look back at him again. He shouts something, looks back at me again.

Aggressive cyclist. Red baseball cap. Oncoming storm. Distant traffic.

Plate glass window. Lime green villa. Folded sun umbrella. Children's trampoline. Red tiles. White walls. Perfect lawn. Empty café. Yellow villa. Green shed. Clipped hedge. Locked letterbox.

Built on the former deathstrip, in the shadow of the Falkensee concentration camp, these houses try to erase history.

Cast iron fence. Italian terrace. Natural stone façade. Dormer window.

*

Concrete blocks. Iron bars. Concrete pillbox. Rampant mistletoe. Steel doors. Narrow windows. Cramped conditions. Meagre diet. Emaciated sculptures. Memorial plaque. Gentle breeze. Slave labour.

Next to a lake, surrounded by fields and trees, one could have built a monastery there.

Exercise yard. Electrified fence. Munitions factories. Steel doors.

*

Newly planted trees. Carved totems. Corrugated cardboard. Dilapidated fence post. Bees collecting pollen. High rise building. Passing cyclists. Wire fence. Further totems. Calling thrush. New housing. Old logs.

No. They are not totems – they show figures, sculpted in wood, climbing the wall.

Paved track. Strangled tree. Passing car. Shot up escapee.

*

Border line. Station grounds. Twisted course. Accessible grounds. Different periods. Complete sections. Brick wall. Electrical installations. Barren clearing. Spontaneous vegetation. Former course. Unusual situation.

Rusted girders of a disused bridge: wall-trellis.

Painted rectangles. Grey frames. Concrete slabs. Shards of glass.

*

Red trunk. Orange fungus. Scots pine. Vacant stare. Sweating jogger. Determined cyclists. Cyclists with all the gear. Sprayed number. Mossy bark. Tall trunk. Dense forest. Fat cyclist.

The distant rumble of a train – or is it thunder?

Freewheeling bicycle. Fit jogger. Competitive executives. Woodpecker.

*

Difficult access. Single track. Complicated course. Small area. Outrageous excuse. Narrow access. Phantom policeman. Reported arrest. Missing schoolboy. Unusual situation. International crisis. Military escort.

The boy claimed he had been arrested by an East German border guard. He'd just been skipping school.

Outrageous excuse. Isolated incident. Difficult access. Complicated course.

*

Dark alley. Crumbling houses. Hollowed bone. White room. Wood stove. Carved figure. Revolving head. Troop carriers. Interesting conversation. Little town. Three soldiers. High window.

After half a year, a year, I wrote a letter asking what was going on, but I didn't get an answer.

Narrow alley. Ice sculpture. Telescopic sight. Emotional object.

*

Broken glass. Smashed glass. White letters. White flag. Severed aorta. Broken glass. Young man. Sallow reality. Forbidden manuscript. Subsidised goods. Bullet-pocked buildings. Baked tile.

It's another unsolved mystery no-one seems in a hurry to unravel.

Long frieze. Grubby windows. Butterfly's wing. Sudden changes.

Patrol track. Sniffer dog. Booby trap. Border guards. Barbed wire. Search lights. Watch tower. Trip wire. Hidden mines. Electric fence. Booby trap. Patrol track.

Seen from above, the border strip looks like a very big and very inviting sandpit.

Impenetrable barrier. Live wire. Hidden mines. Razed spire.

*

Curlicue handlebars. East German jeans. Pop art dress. Florescent blue ice cream. Greasy mullet. Italian circus. Yellow chairs. Red necked skinhead. Short shorts. Empty table. Open filofax. Freewheeling cyclist.

A mother dressed in brown rocks her matching brown buggy to and fro. There is no sign of the child.

Red mohican. Aluminium bin. French lavender. Stunted plane trees.

*

Winged bicycle. Hot sun. German flag. Purple lupins. Dusty track. Painted trees. Bridge barrier. Organised cyclists. Co-ordinated crop-tops. Open goal. Rusting bridge. Purple river.

Stepping on to the trunk road I remember that old joke about elephants.

German flag. Marble wall. Bauhaus design. Forest track.

*

Bored businessman. Bored businessman. Bored businessman. Bored businessman. Bored businessman. Bored businessman. Bored businessman. Bored businessman. Bored businessman. Bored businessman. Bored businessman. Bored businessman.

In sunglasses, on a cord, on a bike, mouth like a handlebar moustache.

Bored businessman. Bored businessman. Bored businessman. Bored businessman.

Other titles from *if p then q*

Tim Atkins. **1000 Sonnets**. 136p. £8.00

Lucy Harvest Clarke. **Silveronda**. 88p. £8.00

Derek Henderson. **Thus &**. 88p. £8.00

Geof Huth. **ntst**. 120p. £8.00

P. Inman. **Ad Finitum**. 114p. £8.00

Tom Jenks. **A Priori**. 80p. £8.00

Tom Jenks. *****. 72p. £8.00

Holly Pester. **Hoofs**. 80p. £8.00

Joy as Tiresome Vandalism. ***aRb* (aR)**. 27p. £10.00

Joy as Tiresome Vandalism. ***aRb* (Rb)**. 17p. £4.00